Original title:
Shadows of the Spruce

Copyright © 2025 Creative Arts Management OÜ
All rights reserved.

Author: Matthew Whitaker
ISBN HARDBACK: 978-1-80567-438-2
ISBN PAPERBACK: 978-1-80567-737-6

Glistening Twilight on Needle Tips

In a forest where pine cones dance,
Squirrels plot their silly prance.
A raccoon with a cap so bright,
Swipes snacks under the moon's soft light.

Elves toss acorns, making a fuss,
While laughter echoes, causing a buzz.
Hooting owls join in the fun,
As shadows stretch, the day is done.

When Dusk Falls on Pine Trails

As the sun dips low and the crickets sing,
A skunk in pajamas does his thing.
He capers and twirls, a sight to see,
While the deer grin, sipping sweet tea.

The hedgehog serves pizza, round on a leaf,
Giggling and jostling, oh what a relief!
Pine needles scatter, a confetti show,
As night creeps in with a cheeky glow.

The Hidden Life of Coniferous Wilds

Beneath the boughs, where no one peeks,
The rabbits hold meetings, not saying a squeak.
They plot little pranks, crafty and spry,
Launching acorns, oh me, oh my!

The playful fox, with a sense of flair,
Wears a scarf made of pine, quite rare!
He juggles with mushrooms, a whimsical sight,
Chuckling, he tumbles, taking flight.

Reveries in a Dimmed Glade

In a glade where the tufts of moss are bright,
A bashful mole plans a picnic tonight.
He invites all his friends, it's quite the affair,
With sandwiches stacked like they just don't care!

The fireflies twinkle, throwing a show,
While turtles play cards—checkmate, oh no!
Laughter erupts, a chorus so grand,
In the heart of the woods, where silliness stands.

Enigmas of the Evergreen Depths

In the forest where the squirrels dance,
A pinecone fell, not by chance.
A raccoon donned a hat of leaves,
As he plotted to steal a few cheese sleeves.

The woodpecker's tap was quite a beat,
A secret club of birds on a street.
But when a rabbit joined the jam,
He forgot his tune, became a sham.

The wise old owl, with glasses on,
Critiqued their style from dusk till dawn.
He hooted loud, 'You call that flair?'
While a crow just laughed, 'You need some hair!'

Beneath the branches, big and bold,
The tales of mischief, silly and old.
In nature's realm, with hugs and cheer,
The forest friends shared laughter here.

Beneath the Twisted Boughs

Beneath the limbs that twist and sway,
The critters gather for a play.
A beaver builds with perfect glee,
While a chipmunk hoards nuts for tea.

The fox rehearses a silly show,
With a hat made of moss, and tails that flow.
The badger grumbles, 'Where's my snack?'
Then trips on a twig, oh what a crack!

The frogs croak songs of ancient lore,
While ants march by, always wanting more.
A beetle's dancing, all around,
While an owl mocks, without a sound.

In this maze of green and brown,
The funny games never wear a frown.
Each twist and turn, a wacky sight,
Creating joy each day and night.

Driftwood Dreams in Darkened Glades

In the glades where secrets sigh,
A hedgehog gave a wink, oh my!
He rolled in leaves, a tiny ball,
While laughing loudly, he made a call.

The driftwood spoke in tales absurd,
Of pirate ships and flying birds.
A rabbit listened, eyes so wide,
Imagining a world where fish could ride.

A turtle, slow but full of wit,
Challenged a snail: 'Let's see who's fit!'
But slipping on moss was quite the jest,
As they both tumbled, laughter blessed.

The night crept in, the stars alight,
Funny shadows danced in the twilight.
In the glades, beneath the beams,
Friendship thrives among silly dreams.

The Lullaby of Timbered Hills

In timbered hills where laughter swells,
A squirrel sang of quirky spells.
His friends would giggle, tails in curls,
As he danced with acorn pearls.

The trees swayed gently, as if to tease,
A rhythm set by the buzzing bees.
A deer tried to join in on the fun,
But tripped on a root, oh, what a run!

The sun peeked through, a golden ray,
Catching a bear who wanted to play.
With a goofy grin and wiggly dance,
He enchanted the crowd, gave laughter a chance.

As crickets chirp their evening song,
In timbered hills, where all belong.
Under the canopy, cheer ignites,
Creating joy in warm, silly nights.

Conversations with the Ancients

In the woods where whispers dwell,
Old trees have tales to tell.
One claimed to spot a ghost,
With a beard, he liked to boast.

The owl said, 'Give me a break!
Those squirrels play for heaven's sake!'
While the raccoons laughed so sly,
'Who needs a ghost? Oh my, oh my!'

The moss agreed, 'Let's eat some cake,
And leave the ghost for nature's sake!'
But all the trees just sat and sighed,
As creatures continued their playful pride.

Between the trunks, the humor soared,
Each ancient mind with wit adored.
They'd sip on dew and chuckle tight,
Underneath the silver light.

Nocturne of the Timbered Solitude

The moon peeked through a fluffy cloud,
The crickets sang, their voices loud.
A fox waltzed in a jaunty way,
Said, 'I'm late, what a dreadful day!'

A badger chortled, full of glee,
'You lost your way while chasing me!'
While shallows thrummed a childish beat,
All creatures danced with fuzzy feet.

The echo of laughter filled the air,
As owls giggled without a care.
They debated if the stars were pies,
And made each other laugh with sighs.

In shadows deep, they spun their tales,
Of silly pranks and gusty gales.
With nature's jest, they welcomed night,
In laughter's embrace, all felt just right.

Reflections in the Boughs

Beneath the bows, the antics grew,
As squirrels performed a funny show.
'Excuse my tumble, how absurd!'
Squeaked one, as laughter softly stirred.

A woodpecker drummed a silly beat,
While beetles joined with tiny feet.
They wove a tale of pure delight,
Of clumsy critters in the night.

'Look at the owl, all wise and grand!
But can he dance, or wiggle his hand?'
Squealed a chipmunk, quick and spry,
Making the moonlight flicker and fly.

The trees nodded with gentle grace,
Each laugh echoing in embrace.
Nature's jesters, bold and free,
Brought joy to all, in harmony.

The Tryst of Twilight Leaves

In twilight's hues, the leaves would sway,
Planning meetings for the next day.
One leaf blushed, 'I've got a date!'
With the breeze, they couldn't wait!

The others rustled with jealousy,
'Why can't we join? Oh let us be!'
But the wind said, 'You'll just pesky rust!
Let romance bloom, then we'll discuss!'

So off they twirled in moonlit grace,
While the branches giggled in their place.
Nature's winks sprawled through the night,
As leaves danced slow, with pure delight.

They whispered jokes, and laughed out loud,
As night cocooned them in its shroud.
From one leaf's wink to another's bounce,
They spun tales, and loved every ounce.

An Ode to Shaded Realms

In the cool, green hideaway,
Silly squirrels play their games,
Hiding nuts in twisted roots,
Pulling pranks with gusty names.

A bird sings a funny tune,
While a bug does a jig below,
They share a bench with mushrooms,
And laugh till the sun says 'Whoa!'

Among the whispers of tall trees,
Giggling branches sway around,
The forest hosts a comedy,
A jester's cloak where smiles abound.

Murmuring Leaves and Ancient Roots

Leaves gossip in the gentle breeze,
Tickling roots that twist and twine,
They tell tales of cheeky deeds,
Of mischievous raccoons divine.

A chipmunk strolls with panache,
Wearing acorns like a crown,
He dances past a sleepy toad,
Who yawns and rolls then plops down!

Fallen pine cones roll and race,
In a contest of woodsy speed,
While old barks chuckle, full of grace,
At nature's comic, joyful creed.

The Cloak of Daybreak's Gracious Light

The dawn light peeks through leafy hats,
Painting the ground with funny hues,
A prankster sun on a rise so bright,
Sparks giggles in morning's shoes.

A fox in shades prances around,
Chasing dreams of shadowed mice,
Tail twitching in daylight's rays,
He thinks he's grown a pair of dice!

The forest giggles at night's retreat,
As daybreak holds its laughter fair,
With critters twirling on bonus beats,
An ode to joy hangs in the air.

Winding Ways and Windy Whims

On winding paths through leafy green,
A journey filled with jest and cheer,
A breeze that tickles at each scene,
Whispers secrets to those who hear.

Round the bend, a feathered troupe,
Perch on branches, ready to jest,
While turtles sashay with modest loop,
A slow-paced dance, they think it's best.

Laughter echoes across the glade,
As twilight falls, the fun won't cease,
With every rustle, new thrills invade,
In this woodland realm of sweet release.

Enshrouded Essence of Nature's Bounty

In the grove where whispers play,
Squirrels plot their nutty sway.
Beneath the bark, a raccoon grins,
Stealing snacks while laughter spins.

A deer trips over roots so sly,
Trying to sneak with a stealthy pie.
The owls hoot a comic tune,
As fireflies dance like a cartoon.

Chipmunks gossip, tails a-twist,
While frogs croak out their own playlist.
A bear arrives, thinks it's a feast,
Only finds a picnic ceased.

Between the trees, there's mischief true,
Nature's jesters in a playful queue.
Laughing leaves, a merry crew,
In this bounty, humor brews.

The Twilight Requiem of the Forest

At dusk, a scene that makes you smile,
A beetle playing hide-and-seek awhile.
With each rustle, the critters tease,
Catching fireflies with carefree ease.

Bats swoop low, they're quite the sight,
Chasing moths like it's a dance at night.
A hedgehog rolls in berry bliss,
Dreaming of a sweet, juicy kiss.

Night birds squawk their jokes of yore,
While the moon grins, wanting more.
In the woods where fun won't cease,
Nature's laughter, a pure release.

Familiar whispers trace the air,
A jolly chorus with nary a care.
The stars wink, join in the game,
As the forest revels without shame.

Indiscernible Patterns in the Glade

Patterns rise in nature's art,
A wiggly worm plays its part.
With each squirm, it giggles loud,
While bees buzz by, feeling proud.

Mushrooms look like hats for ants,
As they host uninvited dance.
A chipmunk prances in wild glee,
Hiding acorns for a spree.

Blades of grass sway to a beat,
Grasshoppers jump, quick on their feet.
A rabbit bumps into a tree,
Rubbing ears, oh such a spree!

Throughout the glade, a puzzled hue,
Nature's comedy, a charming view.
In twisted branches, laughter blooms,
As every critter finds its room.

Canopy of Dreams and Reflections

High above, the leaves conspire,
Whispering tales around the fire.
A snugly owl with glasses round,
Reads the dreams that swirl around.

Beneath the boughs, a party's in,
With ladybugs in a twirling spin.
A fox joins in, red cloak so bright,
Juggling mushrooms, what a sight!

The breeze joins in, a friendly breeze,
Tickling trunks with grand degrees.
Critters chat in a lively row,
While the sun dips low, casting a glow.

In the canopy where fun takes flight,
Every creature feels just right.
As dreams and giggles mix and blend,
Nature's magic never ends.

Phantoms in the Pine Dust

In the grove where shadows play,
The squirrels dance, hip-hip-hooray!
With acorns flying, oh what a sight,
While trees chuckle all through the night.

Raccoons wear masks, oh what a jest,
As they scamper and climb, feeling blessed.
With each twig snapped, they giggle in glee,
Nature's circus, a wild jubilee!

Beneath the Verdant Veil

Mice do cartwheels with such flair,
While crickets play tunes without a care.
Frogs leap in boots that are far too big,
Twirling in splendor—oh, what a dig!

The ferns clap hands for the ladybugs,
As they march in lines with adorable shrugs.
Tickling the air with laughter and fun,
This woodland affair has only begun!

Footfalls on Filigree Ferns

Puddle-jumping with fluffy feet,
The deer breakdance—what a treat!
A leaf drops down, it starts the show,
With whispers and giggles, all to and fro.

A fox in a tie struts down a path,
While badgers join in with a friendly laugh.
Under the stars, inventions arise,
In a dreamy realm where the silly flies!

Spirits of the Misty Copse

Goblins juggling mushrooms with cheer,
Sipping on dew, oh how they steer!
Wandering spirits, they tickle the breeze,
Their laughter echoes through rustling leaves.

A ghost on a swing made of vines,
Swings back and forth, reading the signs.
While owls wear glasses, quite the delight,
In this forest party, all through the night!

Lurking Beneath the Canopies

Squirrels gather, plotting schemes,
While woodpeckers drum silly dreams.
A rabbit hops, with a comedic flair,
Dodging a dance, oh what a scare!

A hiking boot stumbles in glee,
Tripping on roots like it's a spree.
Fallen leaves underfoot snap and crack,
As a turtle lumbers, it's quite a quack!

Laughter echoes through twisted trees,
As chipmunks trade tales with the breeze.
Sunlight flickers, a playful tease,
While shadows wiggle, as if to please!

The forest giggles, it's all a show,
With mother nature in on the pro.
So dance beneath limbs with glee and cheer,
For mischief abounds when friends are near!

Mystery Under the Needle-laden Sky

Underneath the boughs we sneak,
With whispers low and giggles meek.
A bear in pajamas? What a sight!
Even trees chuckle at our delight!

A raccoon wearing sunglasses cool,
Steals our snacks, oh what a fool!
The ferns agree they've seen it all,
As we stumble and laugh, and nearly fall!

Why did the squirrel dash so fast?
Caught in a joke that won't ever last.
The sun peeks through with a knowing grin,
As we chase the tomfoolery hidden within!

Every corner holds a curious twist,
Mistakes that are worthy of a comic list.
Underneath the needle-laden trees,
Where laughter thrives and worries freeze.

The Stillness of Thick Boughs

In the stillness, the giggles start,
A friendly frog plays the trumpet part.
"Ribbit, ribbit, come join my band!"
While a fox claps, ain't life grand?

Among thick boughs, we tell our tales,
Of daring deeds and silly fails.
An owl pretends to be the judge,
While branches shake, just won't budge!

The moon winks down, a cheesy grin,
As shadows jiggle, oh where to begin?
Singing songs from ages past,
Nature's choir, a joyous blast!

When a beetle trips, rolls in the leaves,
We erupt in laughter, oh how it weaves!
The magic lingers, it sweeps us away,
In the stillness where silliness plays.

Hushed Footfalls Among Tall Sentinels

With hushed footfalls, we tiptoe near,
Whispering secrets as friends sincere.
A deer dons glasses, reads the trees,
While squirrels plan a raid with ease!

Each step a giggle, each breath a tease,
Caught in a laughter that's sure to please.
Tanuki dressed up in floral attire,
Twirls around, oh how we admire!

The air is thick with folly and fun,
While fawns play tag and the day's almost done.
Hushed giggles echo, oh what a ball,
As tall sentinels watch over it all!

When night descends, our hearts still bright,
With whispers of joy, we bid goodnight.
So linger with laughter among the trees,
And carry these moments wherever you please!

Flickers in the Twilit Woods

A squirrel in a hat, oh what a sight,
He juggles acorns, quite the delight.
He trips on his tail, with grace so poor,
Lands in a bush, and out flies a spore.

The rabbits are laughing, they start a cheer,
While dancing around with no hint of fear.
Their shadows grow big as they jump and prance,
In a contest of giggles, they take a chance.

A fox in a tux, he joins the parade,
With whispers of mischief, a ruckus made.
He trips on the leaves, slips into a stream,
Turns back to the woods, all soggy, it seems.

But all is undone by a sudden loud crack,
A deer with a trumpet, now that's a fact.
The woods come alive with a musical twist,
Laughter erupts, as the sun starts to mist.

The Dance of Dappled Silence

In the quiet glen, a bear wears a bow,
He leads all the critters in a soft, slow show.
The raccoons clap paws, all in time with the beat,
While the owls look on, showing off their neat feet.

The night sky winks, stars start their play,
A hedgehog in shades gets lost in the fray.
He trips on a twig, but laughs in surprise,
As fireflies flash like stars in their eyes.

A turtle joins in with a slow, drawn-out jig,
He twirls on his shell, feeling quite big.
The laughter erupts, echoing through the place,
As the moon shines bright, casting smiles on each face.

The fun never ends; it's a whimsical ride,
Where even the shadows just bounce and glide.
In dappled light's grip, they sway and they spin,
In a forest of merriment, they all can win.

Ghosts Among the Needles

The wind whispers secrets with a mischievous tune,
While a sprite with a giggle floats past the full moon.
She's playing a game with the shadows around,
As they dance through the trees, making nary a sound.

A ghost wears a bed sheet, but clearly has flair,
He trips on a root, sends a squirrel in the air.
With a sigh and a laugh, he admits with a grin,
He'll stick to his haunting, but never to win.

The owls look bemused and the bats start to swoop,
While the trees all chuckle, this wild, silly group.
They join in the jest; the night turns to glee,
As the haunts of the woods choose to just let it be.

With a final encore, the sprites bid goodbye,
Leaving echoes of laughter under the night sky.
In a forest of whimsy, they wave with delight,
As the ghosts and the creatures say, "What a night!"

Where Sunlight Meets Shade

A chipmunk on a swing, oh what a thrill,
He yells to the sun, "Let's play, if you will!"
With the breeze in his fur and a wink in his eye,
He flips through the air, nearly touching the sky.

The shadows grow long, as the sun starts to sink,
While a raccoon on a seesaw begins to think.
He rides to the top, but takes quite a fall,
Landing right next to a very fat stall.

The ants on parade march straight through the shade,
With little top hats, they strut, unafraid.
A ladybug twirls, shines bright in her grace,
As the laughter erupts, filling up the space.

With a flick and a flap, the dragonflies zoom,
While the sunbeams curve low, brightening the gloom.
In a world where they frolic, so joyful and free,
The woodland ensemble lives life with glee.

The Veiled Dance of Pine Shadows

In the forest deep, they prance,
Swaying branches in a trance.
They giggle as they brush the floors,
While squirrels plot their tiny wars.

The breeze tickles their leafy cheeks,
Mischief hides where nature sneaks.
Quite the pair, the bark and bough,
Doing the limbo, oh wow wow!

They whisper secrets, soft and low,
Telling tales of long ago.
The whispers turn to laughter loud,
As beetles join the merry crowd.

A dance-off with the sun's bright rays,
Twisting limbs in playful ways.
And while the night begins to fall,
The branches bow in curtain call.

Echoes of Dreams Beneath Tall Loblollies

Beneath the boughs, the critters scheme,
Barking jokes and living dreams.
The rabbits waltz, the owls groove,
While dragonflies burst into a move.

A raccoon plays a tiny drum,
While frogs croak out a silly hum.
The tall trees sway and jiggle too,
As if they've caught this dance-flu!

In the twilight, they form a line,
Each leaf shaking, feeling fine.
With every twist, they tease the night,
Tickling stars in sheer delight.

And when the dawn peeks through the pines,
They giggle at their nightly signs.
"Let's do it all again," they shout,
As woodpeckers dance with no doubt!

Starlit Whispers in the Timber

Underneath the twinkling skies,
The tallest trees spread wide their thighs.
They flap their arms, they stomp their feet,
As raccoons jam to a funky beat.

A swing from branch to branch they take,
As fireflies buzz, a glowing flake.
The owls hoot, "Let's start a show!"
With forest critters all aglow.

The air is filled with laughter bright,
As shadows dance in sheer delight.
With every crack, a new surprise,
As lines of laughter fill the skies.

Vines twist and twirl, in leaps they twine,
Tangled feet in a boisterous line.
And as day breaks with the golden sun,
Each tree exclaims, "What funky fun!"

Secrets Entwined in Twisted Roots

Deep in the earth, where roots conspire,
They play like children, never tire.
Tangled limbs and giggles rise,
With whispers sweet, beneath the skies.

The gnarled roots wiggle with delight,
As rabbits hop in the soft moonlight.
With every rustle, stories spring,
Of all the nonsense that they bring.

A squirrel juggles acorns stout,
While the trees laugh and twist about.
With leafy hats, they play charades,
And tease the deer who peek from glades.

As dawn arrives, their giggles stay,
In playful rounds, they greet the day.
Twisted roots and leaves on high,
In this wild place, they'll always lie.

Whispers Beneath the Evergreen

Beneath the boughs, the squirrels chat,
Discussing who stole the garden mat.
The raccoons giggle, hiding their finds,
As laughter echoes through the vines.

A rabbit trips on a knotty root,
Wearing a shirt that's far too cute.
The foxes wink, with a knowing glance,
While a hedgehog joins in, ready to dance.

A party breaks out under green skies,
With pinecone hats and joyful cries.
The woodpecker's beat keeps the rhythm tight,
As the critters celebrate under moonlight.

When night comes rolling, shadows prance,
A raccoon in boots leads the woodland dance.
With every stumble, it's giggles galore,
In the whispers of trees, laughter will soar.

Secrets of the Silent Thicket

In the thicket, secrets swirl,
A singing beetle makes my head twirl.
A dragonfly dances on a twig,
While a frog croaks out a jaunty jig.

A snail boasts of his slow, grand race,
Saying, "I'm winning, just give me space!"
The squirrels roll eyes, with a sly little grin,
As they gather acorns, planning their win.

The owls hoot softly, sharing old tales,
Of hilarious chases and nutty fails.
The mouse with a cheese hat gives a cheer,
In this leafy patch, laughter is near.

When twilight falls, the thicket comes alive,
With all of its critters eager to strive.
They chatter and chuckle until the moon's glow,
In the gentle night air, friendship will grow.

Dance of the Dusky Pines

Beneath the pines, where the giggles arise,
A chipmunk in boots shows off his surprise.
With each little leap and comedic flop,
The laughter echoes, it never will stop.

The wise old owl begins a tale,
Of a squirrel's mishap and the wind's wild gale.
As the trees sway, the pines join in,
Rustling their needles, a dance to begin.

A raccoon rolls over, bursting with glee,
As he tumbles and spins, oh what a spree!
With his little friends all giggling away,
In the dusky light, they frolic and play.

When the stars peek down, it's a jovial sight,
The woodland creatures laugh 'til the night.
Dancing and dreaming beneath the tall trees,
In a merriment that travels with the breeze.

Echoes in the Forest Glow

In the forest glow, echoes of fun,
A fox with a hat is on the run.
Chasing its tail with a whimsical flair,
As the laughter cascades through the air.

The beavers plan a wild, grand feast,
With a potato sack race, they won't be least.
Ducks cheer them on with their flapping delight,
While the bushy-tailed crew takes flight.

The porcupine dons a flower crown,
In her prickly way, she twirls around.
A jolly old turtle makes his own way,
With a slow-motion dance that'll brighten the day.

As evening colors paint the sky's dome,
The creatures find joy in their woodland home.
They gather together, under stars' gleam,
Beneath the tall trees where laughter will dream.

Lost in the Canopy's Embrace

In a world of leafy green,
I lost my way, - it was quite the scene.
A squirrel laughed, clutching a nut,
While I tripped over roots in a rut.

Branches tickled as I passed below,
The dancing leaves put on a show.
A curious bird chirped with glee,
"You're a guest in my home, just wait and see!"

I stumbled and tumbled, oh what a trip,
Pinecone projectiles made me flip.
Laughter echoed, came from above,
Even the trees seemed to share the love!

With every step, a giggle found,
Nature's jokes abound all around.
So here I roam, in this playful land,
And join in the fun with a clumsy hand.

Hushed Histories of the Underbrush

In whispers low, the ground confides,
Tales of mischief where humor resides.
An ant in a tuxedo slipped on a leaf,
"Life's a party!" he sang, quite the chief.

Under the ferns, the beetles joked,
"I'm the fastest!" one proudly stroked.
But slipped on dew, what a dismiss,
Landing headfirst, into a flower's abyss!

Mice played tag with their cheese-shaped hats,
Dodging the fox who nibbled on pats.
Each flower giggled at the ruckus below,
Nature's laughter always on show.

So listen close to the quiet ground,
For in the stillness, mirth can be found.
Every rustle and shuffle brings cheer,
In the underbrush, stories appear.

Tapestry of Shadows and Breezes

A breeze flutters by, tickling my ear,
As shadows sketch stories, far and near.
An acorn dropped, plunked on my head,
I laughed it off, it's the spirit instead!

The wind howled jokes through the open air,
Whispered secrets in the knots of hair.
A rabbit bounced by, wearing a hat,
"Have you seen my carrot? It's under the mat!"

The trees swayed and danced in delight,
Leaves doing the cha-cha, oh what a sight!
With laughter erupting from every bough,
Living portraits, amusing somehow.

As twilight falls, the giggles remain,
Even the night critters play their refrain.
In this woodsy tavern, we treasure the fun,
In every whisper and play of the sun.

Tales Told by the Whistling Wind

With a whoosh and a whistle, the wind did speak,
"Listen closely, my friend, for laughter we seek!"
A breeze tickled branches, so playful and spry,
Teasing the leaves with a gleeful sigh.

A timid hedgehog waltzed on the path,
Doing his dance, inciting the laugh.
"Roll with it, pal, just let it all out!"
The wind joined in with a whooping shout!

Acorns fell softly, a "thud" and a roll,
Making the forest giggle, oh what a goal!
A raccoon peeked out, in mid-nap surprise,
"Is it snack time already?!" he brightly cries.

The tales spun wild, around every bend,
With each gust of wind, a new twist to send.
So dance with the breezes, let laughter unwind,
For humor's the secret, in whispers we find.

Renewal in the Shadows of Growth

In the forest where laughter calls,
The trees share secrets, the squirrel sprawls.
A playful nudge from a twig on the toe,
"Oops! Sorry, friend!" – a leafy throw.

The mushrooms giggle as they sprout,
While rabbits race with a joyful shout.
A dance of ferns in the gentle breeze,
Tickling the knees of the shyest trees.

Sunlight peeks through, it's a cheeky glance,
While acorns band together for a brave stance.
"Let's play tag!" chirps the sprightly crew,
As pinecones tumble on a game, brand new.

So here we gather, each tall and stout,
In growth's embrace, there's no doubt.
With jests and japes, nature's delight,
In the rustling giggles, we take flight.

Forest Told Stories in the Dark

When dusk arrives, the forest chuckles,
As nightingale sings to frolicsome snuggles.
The owls clear their throats, then share,
"Remember the time? Oh, what a scare!"

With chuckles of crickets, they spin their tales,
Of cheeky ants on their wobbly trails.
"Did you see the badger in his new tie?"
"All dressed up, but oh my, oh my!"

The pines lean in with a creaking sigh,
"We danced with the fog, oh how we did fly!"
Under the moon's watchful, playful eye,
The trees share laughter, the stars wink high.

So around the campfire, stories run wild,
In the whispering dark, we're all the child.
With giggles and glee, the forest delights,
In the shimmer of night and the thrill of heights.

Elders of the Evergreen Whispering

The elders of green sway gently around,
While squirrels in jackets do pirouette down.
"Dear branches!" they caw with a wrinkled grin,
"We've seen the seasons; let the pranks begin!"

"Who's tangled in vines? Oh, what a sight!"
The moss-covered stones are rolling with fright.
"Watch your hats, folks," the old oaks will say,
"For the wind loves to lift them and whisk them away!"

"Remember last spring?" the spruce softly quips,
"When the birds threw a party with sweet honey sips?
The raccoons in tuxedos stole quite the show,
While the fireflies danced, putting on quite the glow!"

In these wise woods where mischief abounds,
The laughter rings out with joyous sounds.
For even the wise need a good hearty laugh,
In the moments of whimsy, we share their path.

Ephemeral Glimpses Through the Thick

Through tangled limbs, the sunbeams peek,
While cheeky critters play hide and seek.
"Come find me!" squeaks a nimble hare,
As the thickets chuckle, without a care.

A flash of orange – it's a fox with flair,
Twisting and twirling like he just don't care.
"Did you see that?" gasps a startled bird,
Nature's merry pranksters, oh how absurd!

The glowworms waltz in a silvery stream,
Joining the party in a bright little beam.
With giggles and hops, the woods come alive,
Celebrating the buzz of this vibrant hive.

In the depths of the thick, where moments are rare,
Laughter erupts like the freshest air.
For in this wild world, play is the key,
To unveil the magic and just let it be.

Whispers of the Dense Thicket

In the brush where the wild things play,
A squirrel slipped, thought it was ballet.
Rabbits giggled, dressed in leaves,
Plotting tricks up their furry sleeves.

A raccoon with a pie was caught,
Claimed it was his gourmet thought!
The owls hooted jokes all night,
As forest friends took flight in flight.

When the moonlit party got wild,
A deer danced like a carefree child.
Branches swayed, they joined the waltz,
Until a storm caused all to halt!

"Oh no!" cried the hedgehog in fear,
"Here comes the rain, it's time to steer!"
They scattered fast, a comedic scene,
In the thicket, nature's dream team!

Chiaroscuro in the Grove

In the grove where sunlight plays,
Monkeys swing in mischievous ways.
A fox in shades, swaying fine,
Making shadows dance in a line.

The sun peeked through the leafy greens,
Spotlighting squirrels in their routines.
"Catch me if you can!" they taunted loud,
As the oak trees laughed, feeling proud.

A hare with style wore a vest,
Judged the others; who looked best?
When crickets chirped a catchy tune,
Even the trees swayed, feeling the groove!

With a flick of his tail, the fox took flight,
Gathered his pals for a dance that night.
In the chiaroscuro, the laughter soared,
Mirth and mischief deeply adored!

The Stillness of the Timber Heart

There's a peace in the wood, so sweet,
Where birds conspire to gossip and greet.
A bear tried yoga by a stream,
Cada pose led to a splashing dream.

The bark beetles tapped a beat,
As chipmunks pulled off a grand retreat.
Each branch quivered with laughter loud,
Making humor a part of the crowd.

When the crickets staged a comedy show,
Even the owls had to let it flow.
"No hooting, please! We want to hear,
The punchline that brings us cheer!"

As night enveloped the timber heart,
Creatures chuckled, each played their part.
In the stillness, joy took its flight,
And the woods echoed their pure delight.

When the Pines Hold Their Breath

When pines leaned closer, all stayed hush,
A woodpecker caused quite a rush!
"Did you hear that joke?" one squirrel teased,
While all the branches momentarily ceased.

The beavers built a dam of delight,
Kicked back to watch nature's comedy night.
"Who's got the best laugh?" the owl inquired,
And the forest erupted, laughter inspired!

With a rattle and hum, the critters convened,
A raccoon's tall tale left all in a gleaned.
When laughter rang out, the pines would sway,
In their stillness, they'd chuckle and play.

So when the pines hold their breath in delight,
Nature warms up, ready for flight.
In every rustle, a giggle would bloom,
For fun was alive in the forest's room!

Veils of Pine and Moonlight

In the night, the trees all dance,
Whispers float with every chance.
Squirrels giggle, running about,
Chasing shadows, there's no doubt.

Beneath the branches, secrets peek,
Owls hoot softly, quite unique.
The pinecones fall like tiny bombs,
Making mischief with their charms.

Raccoons throw a late-night feast,
Nibbling snacks, they won't be ceased.
Branches sway, they make a show,
As if in on the midnight glow.

Laughter ripples through the dark,
Nature's jest, a playful spark.
In the veil where shadows creep,
The funny tales, they never sleep.

Echoes in the Forest's Embrace

Under the boughs, the secrets hide,
Mice in suits, good at disguise.
Chirping birds, they crack a joke,
While lazy bears just groan and poke.

Leaves giggle with a gentle breeze,
Swaying and playing, oh, what tease!
The brook gurgles with laughter so bright,
As frogs jump high in pure delight.

Each rustle tells a tale so sly,
Of sneaky foxes and a pie,
It vanished fast with just one snap,
Turns out, it kissed the raccoon's cap.

The forest chuckles, a merry choir,
Nature's wit, a secret fire.
Between the trees, the spirits play,
Echoing fun, come what may.

The Gloom Between the Trees

In the gloom where creatures plot,
Bunnies hop and squirrels trot.
A spider spins a web of fun,
Caught in giggles, then they run.

The moonlight peeks, quite a delight,
Illuminates the comical sight.
Leaves whisper jokes in rustled tones,
As crickets chirp in silly moans.

A lost raccoon with a missing shoe,
Scratches its head, what to do?
While owls roll their eyes in spite,
At clumsy antics in the night.

Mushrooms sway like they own the place,
With toadstools dancing, a silly race.
Each step echoes with glee and cheer,
In the gloom, there's nothing to fear.

Murmurs of Forgotten Trails

On forgotten paths, the giggles roam,
A bear in pajamas claims his home.
Twirling flowers with hats askew,
Nature's circus, what a view!

Beneath the oaks, the shadows play,
Tales of mischief come out to sway.
A rabbit slips on a slick old root,
Land's a laughter, oh, what a hoot!

Murmurs drift on a playful breeze,
Squirrels barter with toasted cheese.
Fireflies twinkle with giddy delight,
Winking secrets in the night.

Through leafy halls, the fun unfolds,
Of snickering crickets and treasures untold.
Every turn reveals a smile,
In the woods, let's linger a while.

Veil of the Sultry Canopy

Under leafy wigs, the critters prance,
Squirrels in tuxedos flaunt their dance.
Beneath the branches, a gecko sings,
Chasing pollen like a bee on wings.

Frogs wear hats made of acorn shells,
While owls throw parties with jolly yells.
The rustling leaves giggle in delight,
As fireflies twirl, shimmering bright.

Gnomes sneak in, playing hide and seek,
Tickling the ferns, oh, what a cheek!
With every bump and every shout,
Nature's laughter echoes all about.

At dusk they toast with berry wine,
While dancing with shadows, oh so fine.
In the veil, the night does sway,
The mischief blooms, come what may!

Silhouettes in the Twilight Grove

In the dusk, the vines entwine,
Creatures weaving tales divine.
With every laugh, a beetle dons,
A tiny crown as the night responds.

Mice in cloaks chase the twilight,
Their tiny giggles a joyous sight.
The moon plays peek-a-boo above,
As stars wink down, in love.

Balloons made of dandelions fly,
Chasing a breeze, oh me, oh my!
Foxes with tipsy tails dance around,
Through giggling grasses they are found.

A flute made from a pinecone shared,
While owls hoot laughs, none are scared.
Underneath the moon's soft glow,
The humor of nature begins to flow.

Murmurs Amongst the Firs

Whispers bounce off the sturdy trees,
Oh look, what's that? A dog in knees!
Pine needles tickle the chattering crowd,
As chipmunks gossip, all too loud.

Bristlecones wear a vibrant hat,
While critters dance, so sleek and fat.
Hares tell tales of daring feats,
While dancing ants share their sweet treats.

Caterpillars, all decked in fluff,
Sway to the rhythm, that's their stuff.
Every wiggle, a boisterous cheer,
Inviting all close, far and near.

With laughter fresh as the morning dew,
Nature's concert is quite the view.
In among the firs, fun never sleeps,
Jokes and giggles, in nature's keeps.

Enigmatic Aromas of the Wood

In the woods, a scent so sweet,
Mushrooms party, quite the feat!
With wafts of cedar and hints of pine,
Even the raccoons sip their wine.

Giggling vines climb high and lush,
As ants compete in a joyful rush.
Bears in aprons bake their pies,
Under bright and twinkling skies.

The air is filled with playful tease,
As porcupines swirl like autumn leaves.
Dancing around in olfactory bliss,
A bouquet of laughter you can't miss.

As dusk arrives with colors bright,
The woods take on a comical light.
Enigmatic aromas, laughter, and cheer,
In this wild retreat, there's nothing to fear.

Moonlit Musings Beyond the Pines

In the glade where raccoons start,
A moonlit dance, a squirrel's art,
The owls hoot jokes, a nightly spell,
While fireflies giggle, they know it well.

A deer in shades, so shy and coy,
Trots on twigs like a merry boy,
With whispered laughs, the winds conspire,
To lift the pine dust, a wacky choir.

The crickets chirp a serenade,
As pine cones roll, a grand parade,
They tumble, trip, and gleefully tease,
While moonbeams dance with dapper ease.

Here nature plays a silly game,
Each creature steps, nobody's tame,
In this wild, whimsical reprise,
The night unfolds, where laughter flies.

The Call of the Dusk Dweller

At dusk, the critters start their show,
A raccon's hat, a real night pro,
They plot mischief in the cool grass,
While shadows twist, a laughing mass.

The hedgehog rolls like a ball of fun,
While owls trade puns, till day is done,
A fox prances, in style it struts,
Wearing a smile that surely cuts!

Beneath the boughs, a party brews,
A squirrel with jokes and funny news,
The pines nod as if in a trance,
While moles dig under, joining the dance.

With a banquet of nuts and dew-kissed treats,
The night creatures gather for comic feats,
In this woodland realm, so unrefined,
Where laughter reigns, and fun's intertwined.

Subtle Echoes of Lost Paths

In the thicket where giggles roam,
The shadows sway, a hidden home,
A fox with wit, sharp as a tack,
Cracks mischievous puns, never lack.

With pine needles' tickle, they burst with glee,
As fawns trip lightly, oh what a spree,
A grouse struts by, feathers all fluffed,
In the party of dusk, where craziness's stuffed!

The moon peeks through, with a cheeky grin,
As toads croak jokes with a devilish spin,
The rustle of leaves, a laughter parade,
While creatures band together, no plans to evade.

In secret corners, the night takes flight,
With silly secrets hidden from sight,
Through the woodland trails, the laughter beams,
In the dance of the night where nonsense gleams.

Beneath the Canopy's Enigma

In the forest where whispers creep,
Squirrels confer, secrets they keep.
Branches dance with a comical sway,
While branches join in a woodland play.

A raccoon wears a mask on its face,
Claiming it's there just for the chase.
Twigs snap underfoot, causing a stumble,
Amidst the giggles, trees seem to rumble.

Mushrooms giggle with a sprightly glee,
As a frog leaps, tries to tease a bee.
The sunlight plays tricks, flickering bright,
Convert the mundane into sheer delight.

Under leaves that seem to chuckle and sway,
Nature's jesters in a lively display.
With laughter echoing from trunk to root,
The woods become a whimsical loot.

Silhouettes of Earth and Sky

In playful forms, the branches twist,
As shadows dance—none can resist.
A fox dons boots to prance through glades,
Wearing a grin amidst leafy cascades.

Blue jays gossip with quite a flair,
Chattering secrets floating in air.
A rabbit hops in a jaunty jig,
While the owls hoot, all wise and big.

Drifting clouds look down to jest,
As if judging each creature's quest.
Beneath, the squirrels launch a nut,
Retrieving the prize with a comical tut.

Life's a circus, a grandeur show,
Where nature's actors steal the glow.
In this realm of mirth and play,
The world outside just fades away.

Hidden Realms Amongst the Foliage

Nestled deep where mischief brews,
Gnomes tiptoe with polka-dot shoes.
Bushes giggle as rabbits prance,
Beneath the leaves, everyone has a chance.

A hedgehog rolls, seeking a snack,
While butterflies twirl in a quirky hack.
Frogs wear crowns in their pondy feast,
Claiming their realm with whimsical cheek.

As daisies debate who's the fairest flower,
Frisky squirrels, plotting in tower.
They toss acorns in a playful spree,
With each little plop, there's glee to decree.

In the hum of life, laughter takes flight,
As creatures conspire from day into night.
Unseen antics, in woodland views,
With every rustle, nature renews.

Saffron-tinged Dusk Under the Pines

As day drifts low, the trees tease light,
In bustling whispers, they prepare for night.
A tiny owl attempts to sing,
But ends up stuttering in a flapping fling.

Caterpillars groove on branches so grand,
Wobbling like they've a band at hand.
Stars peak out, wearing twinkling hats,
While bears roll by, engaged in their chats.

Fireflies twinkle, a disco blur,
As raccoons frolic, in mischief they stir.
The moon joins in, a bright alloy,
With a grin that spreads the night's pure joy.

In every crackle, a giggle's due,
As the pines sway 'neath the dusky hue.
Underneath the twilight's shrill hymn,
The woods are laughing, their edges brim.

Silent Majesties in the Narrow Wood

In the quiet forest, trees stand tall,
Whispers of giggles, as bark starts to squall.
Squirrels trade tales, with acorns in hand,
While branches debate who will make the grand stand.

With mossy green hats and roots that wiggle,
The trees have a laugh, oh how they giggle.
A nut falls down, it causes a scene,
As critters collide, in this living routine.

Old trunks can tell jokes from ages gone by,
Where pinecones drop puns, oh my, oh my!
The air is alive with a ticklish breeze,
As laughter erupts among the tall trees.

The Play of Light on Thick Trunks

Sunlight dances on the bark's tough skin,
Making funny shapes, like a circus within.
The woods hold a jest, as shadows parade,
While twigs crack a smile in nature's charade.

Leaves shake with laughter, such a charming sight,
Casts of mischief that play with the light.
A tree's playful wink catches the sun,
As beams throw a party, nature's great fun.

Underneath the boughs, the ground starts to chuckle,
With each little rustle and twinkling muckle.
The thickest of trunks, bearing secrets so sweet,
Flaunt their wise cracks in the rhythm of feet.

Veils of Mist in Forest Halls

Wandering through fog that tickles your nose,
The trees wear their secrets like whimsical clothes.
Mist giggles softly, a crafty disguise,
As wanderers wait, with wide-open eyes.

See how the ferns in the fog are so sly,
They wink at the toadstools that float nearby.
Whispers of humor drift through the air,
As frisky young critters dart here and there.

Old trees are jesters, with branches like arms,
Swinging and swaying, sharing their charms.
The mist swirls around, creating a scene,
Where laughter and fog blend, a playful routine.

When Pines Hold Their Breath

When the pines hold their breath, it's a sight so absurd,
They look like they're plotting, the tallest, the stirred.
As laughter erupts from the critters below,
These evergreen guardians put on quite a show.

A dance in the breeze, with their needles alight,
Branches throw shade while they take a quick flight.
The forest erupts like a merry surprise,
With chuckles from creatures beneath their wise eyes.

Each sapling giggles, a mischievous feat,
As pinecones do cartwheels, oh isn't it neat?
Nature holds court, with the funniest guests,
When the pines hold their breath, jesters are blessed.

The Murmuring Heart of the Forest Night

In the deep, dark woods where the creatures creep,
A squirrel threw acorns, fell fast asleep.
Owls traded jokes, oh what a delight,
While raccoons danced under the shimmering light.

The trees had a giggle, their branches did sway,
As the moon pulled a prank on a deer, so cliché.
The stars winked in chorus, a mischievous crew,
Drafting plans for a party, just not for you!

A bear told a tale, one mixing up facts,
Of a bee that could howl, surprising all his pals.
Frogs croaked in laughter, their chorus a mess,
In the murmur of night, joy's all that's expressed.

So when you meander, don't go out alone,
The woodland is rich with a humor well-known.
Bring back a good story, let it take flight,
In the heart of the forest, it's always a sight.

Beneath the Twilight's Sway

Beneath the soft glow, in the dusk's light embrace,
Tall pines shared a secret, giggles we could trace.
Hedgehogs played cards with a trickster raccoon,
While the toads held a concert, oh what a tune!

The fireflies flashed like a neon display,
As chipmunks debated who'd win in a race.
Their tiny paws pittered, they zipped 'round in packs,
Trading jokes in a language, only they had the hacks.

A fox in a bowtie presented his style,
With a wink and a smirk, he invited a smile.
All the critters laughed, oh, what a scene,
Under twilight's sway, life felt like a dream.

So join in the fun, wherever you roam,
Nature is lively, it's far from alone.
Find joy in the whispers the branches will say,
As the night twirls and dances, in its own unique way.

Whispers Beneath Evergreen Canopies

Beneath the green boughs, where the secrets are found,
A possum slipped by with a laugh so profound.
Squirrels held meetings, their plans full of beans,
While crickets performed in their shiny-green jeans.

A badger was painting with berries, how bold,
He made quite a mess, but the stories were gold!
The shadows were prancing, with glee in the air,
As a turtle spun tales of past a day rare.

The bushes convulsed with each peal of glee,
Spying on antics, as wild as can be.
The wind was a jester, playing tricks on the trees,
While owls, in the dark, kept their chuckles at ease.

So if you hear whispers in the canopy bright,
Know laughter's in bloom, and all's set just right.
Wander through moments where giggles unite,
In the dance of the forest, everything feels light.

Secrets of the Silent Grove

In a grove that's so silent, secrets play hide,
A hedgehog named Harold took everyone for a ride.
With each little rustle, a tickle, a tease,
Laughter swelled tall on the soft summer breeze.

The owls, wise and crafty, devised a big scheme,
To host a grand party beneath the moonbeam.
They decked out the branches in silly, bright hues,
And invited the critters with colorful cues.

Bunnies danced clumsily, the frogs croaked with cheer,
As the moon took its place, like a spotlight so dear.
The trees joined the jive, their trunks shimming wide,
In the heart of the grove, joy was the guide.

As dawn painted sky with the light of the day,
The whispers grew quiet, but magic won't fray.
So come join the mirth, it's just round the bend,
In the secrets of groves, where all laughter blends.

The Forest's Forgotten Waltz

In the woods where squirrels prance,
A tree stump leads a clumsy dance.
The rabbits clap with furry paws,
While owls just hoot and scratch their jaws.

The mushrooms spin in high couture,
Demanding all their fans demure.
The leaves sway not to music sweet,
But laugh at branches tripping feet.

A bear spins wildly in his role,
Accidentally on a pole!
He grabs a pinecone as a mic,
To serenade the forest bike.

With tippy toes and earnest zeal,
A raccoon shows off a shiny wheel.
The woodland critters cheer so loud,
For nature's dance, they feel so proud.

Veiled Paths in Gloom

Within the woods where shadows lurk,
A hedgehog's laugh is quite the perk.
He tells a tale of mischief bold,
Of wily winds that shake the old.

A fox trots by, all slick and sly,
With tales of snacks that make you cry.
He juggles acorns on his tail,
While toads croak tunes with style and scale.

The mist collects like naughty kids,
Hiding tricks behind the lids.
A raccoon's pranks are reaching high,
While ferns giggle, and branches sigh.

The path is veiled, but don't you fret,
The creatures play with no regret.
In every nook, humor prevails,
While laughter trails on leafy trails.

Beneath the Lofty Pines

Beneath tall pines where echoes flow,
The chipmunks race with quite the show.
They hide their snacks, but what a mess,
They laugh and leap, it's pure excess.

A woodpecker taps a silly beat,
While rabbits groove on happy feet.
They start a band with sticks and stones,
Creating tunes of wacky tones.

A snail, though slow, joins in the jam,
With every note, he's now a fam.
He wiggles and squiggles, a true delight,
Proving humor shines by moonlight.

The breeze carries a jesting tune,
Foretelling laughs, afternoon to noon.
In nature's haven, joy won't cease,
It bounces back with every breeze.

Lanterns in the Greenwood Gloom

In the dark, the lanterns sway,
Glowbugs dance, leading the way.
A raccoon's grin lights up his face,
As he trips over roots in haste.

Mossy carpets are soft and bright,
Where fireflies twinkle, a cheerful sight.
A hedgehog steals a glance and rolls,
To join the fun, oh, furry souls!

The owls hoot with quirky flair,
While whispers tickle through the air.
Each tree a friend, each leaf a clown,
In nighttime's revel, they wear a crown.

Gloom can't hide their merry spree,
For every giggle sets them free.
The woodland glows, not just by light,
But with laughter ringing through the night.

Moonlit Secrets of the Pine Needles

Under the glow of the moon's bright winks,
The pine needles chatter and giggle, it stinks!
A squirrel in a tux struts, oh what a sight,
While raccoons play poker till late in the night.

The owls hoot jokes, their feathers a-fluff,
While pine cones make puns, oh aren't they tough?
A dance party erupts, branches sway with glee,
In this woodland so wacky, no rule is decree.

A fox tells a tale, he's the clown of the crew,
Who knew that a pelt could hide humor so true?
The wind joins the howl like a duo so neat,
Shaking the treetops, a rhythmic heartbeat.

As dawn hints at light, the mischief must end,
The giggles and whispers, they all transcend.
But come back by moonlight, and you will find,
Those pine needle secrets are quite well aligned.

The Interlude of Twilit Pines

In twilight's embrace, the pines gather near,
Their needles like whispers, oh so sincere.
They play hide and seek with the breeze in the air,
And chuckle at shadows escaping everywhere.

The bunnies bring lettuce, a feast for the night,
While chipmunks juggle acorns, oh what a sight!
A fox takes a bow, wearing leaves as his cap,
As the mischievous mice set a trap for the nap.

Each branch holds a secret, a punchline awaits,
A pinecone's quip challenges even the fates.
With laughter like echoes, the twilit array,
Turns serious woods into humorous play.

Just as stars twitch their lights, and crickets join in,
The pines dance with delight, their humor a grin.
As the night fades at last, with a wink and a cheer,
They promise more giggles as the next dusk draws near.

Fables from the Depths of the Wood

Once in a forest where giggles abound,
Tall pines told fables, their laughter profound.
A deer on a skateboard, oh what a show,
While turtles debate on the fastest way to go.

The tales twist and turn like the roots at their feet,
With squirrels on saxophones giving quite a beat.
The porcupine's riddles, a sharp-witted jest,
Leaves everyone guessing, a true comic test.

The trees shared their wisdom, oh funny and wise,
Of how beavers can dance in hilarious guise.
With each rib-tickling yarn, the darkness takes flight,
A forest of laughter, where wrong feels just right.

When the sun claims the sky, the giggles persist,
In every leaf rustle, that humor insists.
So heed the wood's fables, with a chuckle, you'll see,
The pine could outlaugh the best of a spree.

Beneath the Canopy of Whispers

Beneath leafy roofs, where whispers abound,
The jokes travel faster than shadows around.
A gnome with a hat, far too big for his head,
Keeps tripping on roots while the critters are fed.

The trees hold the giggles, the pines to proclaim,
A game of tall tales where all are to blame.
The raccoons eyeing cookies with mischievous glee,
Dropping crumbs for the hedgehogs, quite the spree.

A stream joins the chorus with splashes and smiles,
While frogs in tuxedos perform catwalks for miles.
"Why did the grasshopper hop?" one asks with a grin,
"Because it saw a dog wearing a panty on chin!"

As the stars poke their heads, the laughter takes flight,
The wood holds its secrets, so funny, so bright.
When morning arrives, with sunlight in tow,
The whispers of humor will always bestow.

The Aria of Nature's Serenity

Amidst the trees where whispers dwell,
A squirrel plays with acorn bell.
Dancing leaves in playful hues,
Nature's joke? A squirrel's shoes!

In the breeze, a laughter waves,
While mossy beds hold secret caves.
A rabbit hops, it trips, it rolls,
And giggles echo in the shoals.

The brook hums tunes of nearby dreams,
A fish flips high, or so it seems.
Nature's choir, a symphony,
With critters joining in with glee.

So here we laugh at all we see,
In the green heart of jubilee.
Every twig a funny plight,
In this wood, we dance with light.

Evening Cloaks and Slumbering Spirits

As dusk descends, the owls take flight,
Wearing cloaks of velvet night.
A raccoon with a mask so sly,
Steals a snack and waves goodbye.

The fireflies twinkle, like stars on land,
While frogs recite a croaky band.
With each ribbit, a giggle grows,
Who knew the swamp could put on shows?

A gentle breeze brings tales anew,
Of how the wind can tickle you.
The trees chuckle and sway in jest,
At critters sprawled in evening's rest.

In twilight's arms, all creatures sigh,
Their secret laughs drift through the sky.
For evening cloaks hide more than sleep,
In nature's nooks, the jokes run deep.

The Gaze of Stillness and Solitude

Among the roots, a gopher lies,
Watching clouds with curious eyes.
He dreams of cheese, or maybe pie,
A silent laugh, a happy sigh.

The pine stands tall, it can't help tease,
While lazy bees sip nectar breeze.
In quietude, a whispered jest,
Even the stones are keenly blessed.

A deer tiptoes, thinks herself sly,
Winking sweet at the butterfly.
Stillness wraps the woods in mirth,
Life's little quirks, oh what a worth!

For in the calm, a story weaves,
Of nature's power that never leaves.
In solitude, a smile takes flight,
In the embrace of pure delight.

Knotty Tales of the Wildwood

In tangled woods where mischief thrives,
A rabbit spins and takes a dive.
In search of carrots, what a chase,
He jumps and lands on a squirrel's face!

The oaks all chuckle at the sight,
As playful winds swirl with delight.
A woodpecker drums a silly beat,
And the chipmunks join in, dancing their feet.

Among the vines, a hedgehog grins,
While weaving tales of epic wins.
A flower sways, it takes a bow,
As bees hum tunes, "Hey, how about now?"

These knotty tales of those that roam,
In wildwood's heart, we feel at home.
With laughter echoing in the trees,
Nature spins its yarns with ease.

www.ingramcontent.com/pod-product-compliance
Lightning Source LLC
Chambersburg PA
CBHW071844160426
43209CB00003B/412